DIGITAL WELLBEING FOR KIDS

DR DHEERAJ MEHROTRA

Contents

Preface   *v*

  1. Digital Well-being For Kids   1

  2. Catering To Challenges Of Digital Candy   14

  3. Top 25 Teaching Strategies That Work   24

References: 35

About The Author   37

Books By The Same Author   41

Preface

Digital Well-Being For Kids is a priority for schools and educators. The idea of Digital Well Being is a connect with the kids to explore the best and limited use of digital devices. The researchers say Digital well-being is a term used to describe the impact of technologies and digital services on people's mental, physical, social and emotional health.

It is high time we come together to understand the what and why of Digital Well Being for Kids.

Looking Forward.

Best

www.authordheerajmehrotra.com

I

Digital Well-Being For Kids

What is Digital Wellness?

The concept of digital wellness refers to an intentional state of physical, mental, and social wellness that can be achieved via attentive involvement with both the natural and digital environments.

Concerns among parents and teachers have only increased with the pandemic because students spend more time socialising and learning on their digital devices. Over the years, there has been a lot of hand-wringing about technology's effect on children's social skills and well-being.

Kids are forming their identities, developing relationships, learning to regulate their emotions and actions, and navigating an onslaught of misleading information in this hybrid digital and analogue world. According to a recent poll conducted by Common Sense Media, they are also spending much more time than before the pandemic in the digital media arena. Kids today face new social issues due to social networking, online gaming, virtual learning, and the prevalence of electronic devices.

To what extent do schools teach students the social and emotional skills necessary to thrive in a society increasingly dominated by technology?

While many social and emotional skills kids need to succeed in school and their careers are the same ones they need to be effective digital citizens, technology poses new hurdles.

According to Melissa Schlinger, vice president of practice and programmes at the Collaborative for Academic, Social, and Emotional Learning, or CASEL, students need to be self-aware and can control their emotions. There is a lot of emotionally-charged content on social media, and it encourages people of all ages, including children and adults, to "click first and think later."

According to Kelly Mendoza, vice president of education programmes at Common Sense Media, a nonprofit research and advocacy organisation that also provides curricula and ratings on media and technology, many schools are teaching essential skills such as empathy, taking into consideration the perspectives of others, and managing one's behaviour. The catch is that teachers don't always make the obvious connection between the skills being taught and how students will use technology. Emotional intelligence is a crucial leadership skill for inspiring others to work toward a common objective. Accept and validate their emotions as a way to demonstrate your care.

QUOTE: TOI, Report dt. 23 sept. 2022.

Social media addiction gives you anxiety, depression: US study

Researchers Say That Right After Its Launch, As Facebook Spread In US Colleges During 2004-06, Students Reported Poorer Mental Health

Abhilash.Gaur@timesgroup.com

In August, actor Tom Holland, who plays Spider-Man, announced he was taking a break from social media for his mental health. "I find Instagram and Twitter to be overstimulating, to be overwhelming," he said on Instagram, where he has 68 million followers.

It's a feeling many social media users share, but the fear of missing out (Fomo) and the craving for external validation keep them hooked. Social media observers like Tristan Harris and Zeynep Tufekci have warned about these hooks and their mental-health effects for years. Still, the social networks disagree, claiming the evidence is inconclusive. However, new research published in the American Economic Review claims a strong link between Facebook use and increasing anxiety and depression.

The new study is critical because it correlates two independent data sets from Facebook's early days. Between February 2004 and September 2006, Facebook was gradually rolled out on US college campuses, starting with Harvard. The researchers compared how Facebook's arrival on campus affected students' responses in the National College Health Assessment survey that covers mental health and other well-being issues. When they went over the 4. 3 lakh survey responses from that period, the researchers found "a significant link between the presence of Facebook and a deterioration in mental health among college students," says a report summary by the MIT Sloan School of Management.

The adverse mental health effects were significant: "access to Facebook led to an increase in severe depression by 7% and anxiety disorder by 20%". The researchers estimate Facebook use was about 20% as troubling as losing a job. And this was before Facebook introduced the 'like' button. Another observation was that Facebook's mental health effects grew stronger with time.

Comparative Disadvantage

Psychologists have long believed social-media users feel unhappy because they compare their real lives with their peers' curated virtual lives. This can plunge younger users into depression. Without blaming social media, the US Centers for Disease Control (CDC) says the suicide rate in the 10-24 age group, which was stable from 2000 to 2007, increased by 57% between 2007 and 2017. An article on the University of Utah website says, "Young adults who use social media are three times as likely to suffer from depression – putting a large portion of the population at risk for suicidal thoughts and behaviours. "

Jessica Holzbauer, a clinical social worker quoted in the article, says the filtered, edited and manipulated content posted on social networks like Facebook and Instagram makes some people look good but can negatively affect others' self-image. Some may base their worth on the number of likes they receive and feel disheartened when ignored.

Last year, the Wall Street Journal ran an investigation called 'The Facebook Files' on the social network's "unwillingness or inability" to address its failings. It said researchers within Facebook-owned Instagram knew the network made "body image issues worse for one in three teen girls". According to the WSJ, a more disturbing internal finding was that "Among teens who reported suicidal thoughts, 13% of British users and 6% of American users traced the desire to kill themselves to Instagram."

The team also knew that Instagram's focus on body and lifestyle "can send teens spiralling towards eating disorders, an unhealthy sense of their bodies and depression".

Join the Times Special Readers' Club. Scan the QR code to Young Adults At Greater Risk The question of social media's effect on teen mental health is now in focus as hearing about the 2017 suicide of 14-year-old London girl Molly Russell has just started. Her father, Ian Russell, says Molly killed herself "after viewing 'hideous, graphic, harmful' content on social media sites". The Financial Times reported that "in the months leading up to her death, Molly had viewed a large volume of posts on sites like Instagram and Pinterest related to anxiety, depression, suicide and self-harm."

But even adults find it hard to deal with negativity on social media. As actor Tom Holland says, "I get caught up, and I spiral when I read things about me online, and ultimately, it's very detrimental to my mental state, so I decided to take a step back and delete the app(s)."

There's no doubt that social media has many benefits — connecting with old friends, expanding your professional network, showcasing your work, etc. But if it's telling on your mental health, log off now like Holland.

Source: TOI, https://epaper.timesgroup.com/the-times-of-india/lucknow

II

Catering to Challenges of Digital Candy

Middle school is a turning point for children ages 7 to 13 as they grow more self-reliant and develop more sophisticated Internet use patterns. As an example of potentially harmful behaviour, parents worry that their children may initiate contact with strangers. That's why they must have a conversation about internet safety with them.

A child's Internet use when they enter adolescence is almost inevitable. Most kids today have access to the Internet through a mobile device, and they rely heavily on various social networking sites to maintain and develop their networks of friends. It's getting harder for parents to limit their kids' screen usage.

How well do you know people in common, and who can testify for them?

Interaction With whom would you feel most comfortable interacting with them?

The physical location of the interaction.

Is prior familiarity with the other party(ies) required? What details are they seeking from you, exactly? To what extent are they disclosing or prepared to provide relevant information to you? To consider the other person's perspective: What are they gaining from your conversation? The degree of influence you have over your interactions.

The availability of two-way communication systems is an example of the data covered by this sentence.

It's essential to verify the source. Review the Data, as in Check the Data. Don't Doubt the Data. Disseminating the Data

Third, the impact: how much of a positive or negative effect do your digital habits have on your well-being overall?

Guidance: You should take away from this that your safety depends on the strength of the community in which you live.

This means that the security and well-being of everyone are at risk whenever there is a single point of failure, and this is especially true in a digital setting. This is why it's essential always to be open to new information and continue expanding your knowledge base to promote digital wellness among yourself, your family, and your community.

To sum up, the two most crucial aspects of instruction are

(a) Taking in new information and learning how to use it correctly and

(b) passing on that knowledge to others. a) Instructing Others

Helpful Hints for Educators and Parents

- *Avoid obstructing people from using modern gadgets. Instruct your kid on how to use devices responsibly.*

- *Show interest in your kid's online activity and download their favourite games and applications.*

- *View or make something together at times.*

- *The key is to take on the role of parent. Ultimately, the decision-making rests with you. Restrict access and think about employing technologies to screen inappropriate material.*

- *Put together a family tech usage policy that includes device-free zones like the vehicle, the bedroom, and the dinner table.*

- *Explain to your youngster the dangers of sharing too much personal information in cyberspace (consent of data – online and offline).*

- *Teach your youngster to distinguish between fact and fiction or popularity and accuracy while researching topics online.*

- *Avoid giving a gadget to a youngster as a reward or a present; instead, work through difficult situations together as a family that includes technology.*

- *You should find a happy medium between time spent in front of and away from screens. Prioritize addressing genuine child development issues.*

- *If your child is under 18, you should not encourage them to join sites that require a minimum age of 18. Get educated, check out reputable tools for parents, etc.*

Kids eventually need to learn how to negotiate the highs and lows that are inevitable. For children to grow in their intellectual, social, and emotional independence as well as their physical comfort zones and horizons, it is essential to foster their sense of autonomy. Instil a robust appreciation for the arts, literacy, flexibility, and a strong work ethic in your offspring. These are essential because they have the potential to improve intellect, engagement, and creative expression, all of which may contribute to a greater sense of satisfaction.

III
Top 25 Teaching Strategies that work

Some of the Teaching Strategies with WOW traits within classrooms feature as follows:

1. Lecturing

Lecturing can mean an instructional talk or it can take the form of a stern, one-sided talk. It is in part through engaging students in interaction, using questions and answers, that some of the limitations of lectures can be overcome. The lecture has to be Lively, Educative, Creative, Thought provoking, Understanding, Relevant and Enjoyable.

2. Circle Time Activities

A Circle time, also called group time, refers to any time that a group of people are sitting together for an activity involving everyone. Circle time is usually light and fun and has the goal of getting children ready for learning. Consider the 3 basic questions of Why, What and How.

3. Simulation Method

The system of activating classrooms via Simulations refer as instructional scenarios where the learner is placed in a "world" defined by the teacher. They represent a reality within which students interact. The teacher controls the parameters of this "Engagement" and uses it to achieve the desired instructional results.

4. Modelling Method

The process of Modelling during teaching is an instructional strategy in which the teacher demonstrates a new concept or approach to learning and students learn by observing. Whenever a teacher demonstrates a concept for a student, that teacher is modelling. It activates engagement in real sense.

5. Online Learning Tools

These are the Most Popular Digital Education Tools For Teachers And Learners. The most common ones include Edmodo, an educational tool that connects teachers and students, and is assimilated into a social network. Google Classrooms and Kahoot are other commonly used platforms.

6. Game Simulation

As one of the innovative ways of teaching, the use of simulation games implies that the teacher values the unique needs of individual students. During this process, learning is an active process rather than a passive one. It encapsulates the importance of students' examining their values and the values of others.

7. Collaborative Problem Solving

The very collaborative problem-solving acts as "the capacity of an individual to effectively engage in a process whereby two or more agents attempt to solve a problem by sharing the understanding and effort required to come to a solution and pooling their knowledge and skills in totality. It activates learning by doing hands-on.

8. Discussion Groups

The Discussion method of teaching is a group activity which involves the teacher and the student to define the problem and derive its solution. It is a constructive process consisting of listening, thinking, and deriving conversation skills on priority.

9. Peer Instruction

Peer teaching involves one or more students teaching other students in a particular subject area and builds on the belief that "to teach is to learn twice" (Whitman, 1998)." For students, peer learning can lead to improved attitudes and a more personalized, engaging, and collaborative learning experience, leading to higher achievement. For peer teachers, the experience can deepen their understanding of the subject and impart confidence.

10. Active Learning

Active learning is an approach to instruction that involves actively engaging students with the course material through discussions, problem-solving, case studies, role plays and other methods. The process is towards giving students a time limit to complete the task. The strategy identifies to Stop the activity and debrief. Call on a few students, or groups of students, to share their thoughts and tie them into the next steps of your lecture.

11. Project-Based Learning

Project Based Learning is a teaching method in which students gain knowledge and skills by working for an extended period to investigate and respond to an authentic, engaging, and complex question, problem, or challenge in particular. Project-based teachers ensure that students understand the learning goals and why they matter towards catching them young and innocent.

12. Unit Tests

Unit tests are conducted in the school to evaluate the summative assessment of the teaching-learning process. The main aim of a unit test is to isolate each unit of the system to identify, analyse and fix the defects. The test is different from assessment and evaluation in the following manner towards excellence.

13. Assignments

The Assignment method is the most common teaching method in schools, particularly in teaching science. It is a technique which can be usually used in the teaching and learning process. It is an instructional technique which comprises guided information, self-learning, writing skills and report preparation among the students. It also includes simple homework assignments as a shared learning and evaluation method.

14. Classroom Quizzing and Brain Gym:

Ask questions and make their brain work brighter. Example: Ask them to make the number 9 using their thumb altogether. Ask them to Write their first name in ENGLISH using their index finger in the air.

15. Remedial Teaching

Identify weak students and engage them through peer learning. Involve them through partners as 12.00 O Clock Partners or other time frames. This can even happen before assembly or after school.

16. Presentations

Engage them through presentation skills via Technology. Some widely used presentation platforms include PREZI, MS Powerpoint and KEYNOTE.

17. Zoom In

Let the students observe gradual portions of an image and ask them to write and engage in writing. Ask them what new things they see. How does it change their thinking? Repeat the reveal and questioning until the whole image is revealed.

18. Chalk Talk

Using the Chalk Talk Strategy to engage them via homework analysis. The chalk talk method is an excellent way to ignite shy students. It engages the learners, promotes independent thinking and allows them to have an equal say. Here the teacher tells the students to analyse their thought analysis. The students rotate as a team via different prompts. The output is shared in public.

19. Work Books & Step Inside Routine

It gives the option to students to answer questions using Step Inside virtually. You let them step inside the character of the individuals. It is like stepping inside the situation in particular. Suitable for English, History, and exploring historical events from a specific perspective. Example Thinking or wondering about a soldier's perspective.

20. Posters and Reading Conference

Showcase the Posters and ask the children to read and interact. This goes via interactions randomly with peers and teachers. It integrates Visual Literacy as I see, I wonder. Using posters and the opportunity to read the content individually or as per the lucky system works wonders.

21. Self-Learning Tools

This is a live example of using tools of learning as a practical approach. Some of the online tools include Google Digital Garage, LinkedIn Learning, Coursera, Khan Academy, edX and Academic Earth.

22. Competitions

This includes various formats like Debates/ Interactions/ Recitation/ Writing/ Fashion Shows/ Speech Contests/ Case Study Presentations.

23. Object-Based Learning

Object-based learning is a form of active learning. It is a student-centred learning approach that uses objects to create a more profound learning experience. Is an educational method that involves actively using authentic or replica material things. These objects can include artworks, artefacts, archival materials, or digital representations of unique things.

24. Class Summary

The Class Summary integrates classroom learning via engagement as a priority. To make it effective, the students must first practice the imparted skills of identifying and describing the main topic or activity in a class and giving some coherent, sequenced details. The idea is to catch them young and innocent towards learning as the ultimate.

25. Club Activities

This leads to bodily awareness, independent thinking, problem-solving and reasoning, positive self-image, talent management and collaboration & teamwork. The other activities include co-curricular activities such as public speaking, debate and dramatics, creative writing, eco-club, quizzing, astronomy, dance, photography, philately, trekking, film appreciation and even cooking.

References:

https://telanganatoday.com/cyber-talk-the-need-for-digital-wellbeing-among-kids

About the Author

Dheeraj Mehrotra, MS, MPhil, PhD (Education Management) honoris causa., a white and a yellow belt in SIX SIGMA, a Certified NLP Business Diploma holder, is an Educational Innovator, Author, with expertise in Six Sigma In Education, Academic Audits, Neuro-Linguistic Programming (NLP), Total Quality Management In Education, an Experiential Educator, a CBSE Resource towards School Assessment (SQAA), CCE, JIT, Five S, and KAIZEN. He has authored over 100 books on topics which include Computer Science, AI, Digital Body Language, NLP, Quality Circles, School Management, Classroom Effectiveness and Safety and security in schools. A former Principal at De Indian Public School, New Delhi, (INDIA), NPS International School, Guwahati, and Education Officer at GEMS, Gurgaon, with an ample teaching experience of over Two Decades, he is a certified Trainer for Quality Circles/ TQM in Education and QCI Standards for School Accreditation/ School Audits and Management. He has also been honoured with the President of India's National Teacher Award in the year 2006 and the Best Science Teacher State Award (By the Ministry of Science and Technology, State of UP), Innovation in Education for his inception of Six Sigma In Education by Education Watch, New Delhi and Education World- Best Teacher Award, BOLT Learner Teacher Award by Air India, 'Innovation in Education Award 2016' by Higher Education Forum (HEF), Gujarat Chapter, among others. He has developed over 150 FREE EDUCATIONAL MOBILE Apps for the Google Play Store exclusively for Teachers, Students, and Parents. This work has been recognised by the LIMCA BOOK OF RECORDS & INDIA BOOK OF RECORDS as the only Indian to draw that feast.

Dr Mehrotra works as a PRINCIPAL at KUNWARS GLOBAL

SCHOOL, Lucknow, in India. He has conducted over 1000 workshops globally on "Excellence In Education" integrated with Total Quality Management and Six Sigma, Technology Integration in Education (TIE), Developing towards being ROCKSTAR TEACHERS, including Cyberspace, Cyber Security, Classroom Management, School Leadership & Management, and Innovative teaching within classrooms via Mind Maps, NLP and Experiential Learning in Academics. He is an active TEDx speaker and can be viewed on the youtube TEDx channel.

As a premium UDEMY Instructor, he has developed over 450 courses and caters to over 8 Lakh students from 180 countries.

He can be visited at www.authordheerajmehrotra.com.

BY NATIONAL
AWARDEE
EDUCATOR
Kindle Price: ₹ 72.00
inclusive of all taxes
Teaching in the VUCA WORLD
Dr. Dheeraj Mehrotra
authordheerajmehrotra.com
Flipkart
available at
amazon

BASICS OF
ARTIFICIAL
INTELLIGENCE
&
MACHINE
LEARNING
DR. DHEERAJ MEHROTRA
authordheerajmehrotra.com
Flipkart
available at
amazon
BY NATIONAL
AWARDEE
EDUCATOR
Digital List Price: ₹103.95
Kindle Price: ₹ 99.00
Save ₹4.95 (4%)
inclusive of all taxes

www.ingramcontent.com/pod-product-compliance
Lightning Source LLC
Chambersburg PA
CBHW072044150726
47996CB00014B/1443